Beginner-Friendly Baby Quilts

by Linda Causee

LEISURE ARTS, INC.
Maumelle, Arkansas

Produced by

Production Team

Creative Directors:	Jean Leinhauser and Rita Weiss
Book Design:	Linda Causee
Technical Editor:	Ann Harnden

Diagrams © 2016 by The Creative Partners LLC
Reproduced by special permission

We have made every effort to ensure that these instructions are accurate and complete. We cannot, however, be responsible for human error, typographical mistakes or variations in individual work.

Published by Leisure Arts, Inc.

© 2016 by Leisure Arts, Inc.

104 Champs Boulevard, STE. 100

Maumelle, AR 72113

www. leisurearts.com

Library of Congress Control Number: 2016942646

ISBN: 978-1-4647-5232-2

Introduction

You've just learned that your best friend (favorite aunt, cousin, neighbor or whoever) is soon to become a mother, and you are determined to make the new baby a wonderful quilt. You think you know how to quilt because you've recently learned all of the necessary basics (whether someone taught you, you took a class, or perhaps you taught yourself online).

But now comes the hard part. You feel you may know the basics, and you are sure you can cut and sew the perfect fabric you've found. But all of the patterns you find online, in pattern books or magazines seem too difficult, and the easy ones don't look very attractive.

Here is the answer to all of your problems.

In this book, we've collected some of our favorite patterns that we used in our early quilting days; here you'll find patterns for quilts that we enjoyed making and enjoyed using or were happy to give as gifts.

But—most, most important—all of the quilt patterns are intended for beginners just like you.

And, if you can't remember exactly what you learned, spend a little time with our General Directions on pages 56 to 61. Here we've given you an explanation of how to work all of the instructions we've used in these patterns.

So get started making that quilt for the new baby. You'll not only be glad you did, but you'll be tempted to start making quilts for all those new babies.

Linda Causee

Contents

Tumbling Flowers	6
Hugs and Kisses	10
Whirling Pinwheels	13
Floating Hearts	17
Baby's Log Cabin	20
Baby's Pal	23
Sailing, Sailing...	26
Find the Pinwheels	29
Twirling Flowers	32
Star Galaxy	35
Blocks All Stacked Up	38
Starry Stars	41
Purple Chain	44
Baskets of Love	47
Two Terrific Triangles	50
Pretty in Pink	53
General Directions	56
Template Patterns	62

Tumbling Flowers

Approximate Size: 37" x 37"

What little baby wouldn't love dancing with the leaves and flowers floating across this quilt.

Materials

¾ yd white print

1 ¼ yds med pink print

⅓ yd dk pink print

¾ yd med green print

⅓ yd dk green print

1 ¼ yds backing

batting

Patterns

(page 63)

A Triangle

B Square

Cutting

Note: *Refer to Using Templates, page 57, to make templates and cut fabric.*

Flower Block (8" x 8" finished)

(make 9)

54 A Triangles, white print

9 B Squares, white print

36 A Triangles, med pink print

36 A Triangles, dk pink print

18 A Triangles, med green print

9 B Squares, med green print

18 A Triangles, dk green print

45 B Squares, dk green print

Finishing

2 strips, 2" x 24 ½", med green print (1st border-sides)

2 strips, 2" x 27 ½", med green print (1st border-top and bottom)

2 strips, 2 ½" x 27 ½", white print (second border-sides)

2 strips, 2 ½" x 31 ½", white print (second border-top and bottom)

2 strips, 3 ½" x 31 ½", med pink print (third border-sides)

2 strips, 3 ½" x 37 ½", med pink print (third border-top and bottom)

4 strips, 2 ½"-wide, med pink print (binding)

continued on page 8

Instructions

Making the Block

Sewing the Patches

1. Sew a dk green print A Triangle to a white print A Triangle; repeat for another patch 1. Press seam to one side.

2. Sew a med green print A Triangle to a dk pink print A Triangle for patch 2. Press seam to one side.

3. Sew a med green print A Triangle to a med pink print A Triangle for patch 3. Press seam to one side.

4. Sew a dk pink print A Triangle to a white print A Triangle; repeat for another patch 4. Press seam to one side.

5. Sew a med pink print A Triangle to a dk pink print A Triangle for patch 5. Press seam to one side.

6. Sew a med pink print A Triangle to a dk pink print A Triangle; repeat. Press seam to one side. Repeat for another patch 6.

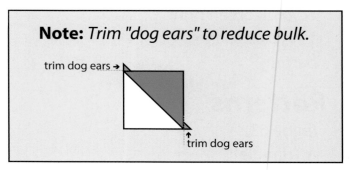

Note: *Trim "dog ears" to reduce bulk.*

trim dog ears →

↑ trim dog ears

Sewing the Rows

1. For row 1, sew together Patch 1, Patch 4, Patch 6 and white print B Square. Press seams to one side.

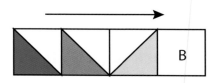

2. For row 2, sew together a dk green print B Square, Patch 2, Patch 5, and Patch 4 together. Press seams in opposite direction.

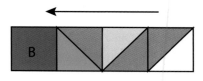

3. For row 3, sew together a dk green print B Square, med green print B Square, Patch 3 and Patch 6 together. Press seams in same direction as row 1.

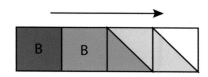

4. For row 4, sew together 3 dk green B Squares and a Patch 1. Press seams in same direction as row 2.

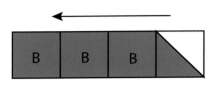

5. Sew rows together to complete block. Make a total of 9 blocks.

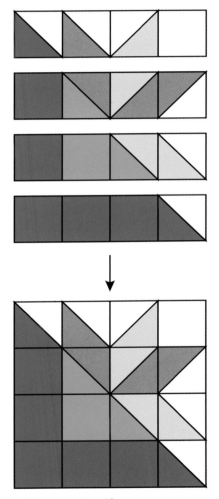

Finishing Your Quilt

1. Place blocks in three rows of three blocks referring to Layout. Sew blocks together in rows, then sew rows together. Press seams to one side.

2. Sew 2" x 24 ½" med green print strips to sides first; press seams toward border. Sew 2" x 27 ½" med green print strips to top and bottom; press seams toward border strips.

3. Sew 2 ½" x 27 ½" white print strips to sides; press seams toward border strips. Sew 2 ½" x 31 ½" white print strips to top and bottom; press seams toward border strips.

4. Sew 3 ½" x 31 ½" med pink print strips to sides; press seams toward border strips. Sew 3 ½" x 37 ½" med pink print strips to top and bottom; press seams toward border strips.

5. Refer to Finishing Your Quilt, pages 58 to 61, to complete your quilt.

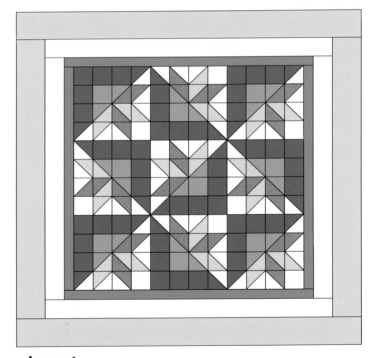

Layout

Hugs and Kisses

Approximate Size 41" x 41"

Like a warm hug, this quilt will embrace that special baby with love.

Materials

⅞ yd blue print
1 ¾ yds pink print
1 ⅛ yds backing
batting

Patterns

(page 63)
A Triangle
B Square

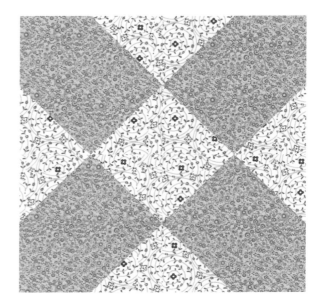

Cutting

Note: *Refer to Templates, page 57, to make templates and cut fabric.*

Hugs Block (8" x 8" finished)

(make 9)

108 A Triangles, pink print
36 B Squares, pink print
108 A Triangles, blue print

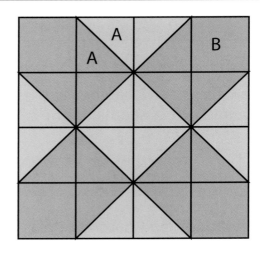

Finishing

2 strips, 2" x 32 ½", blue print (first border-sides)
2 strips, 2" x 35 ½", blue print (first border-top and bottom)
2 strips, 3 ½" x 35 ½", pink print (second border-sides)
2 strips, 3 ½" x 41 ½", pink print (second border-top and bottom)
6 strips, 2 ½"-wide, pink print (binding)

continued on page 12

Instructions

Making the Block

Sewing the Patches

1. Sew a pink print A Triangle to a blue print A Triangle; press seam to one side. Make a total of 12 patches.

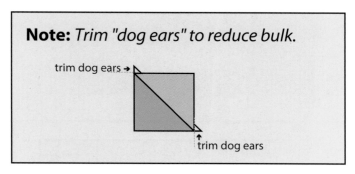

Note: *Trim "dog ears" to reduce bulk.*

Sewing the Rows

1. Sew together 2 patches and 2 pink print B Squares. Press seams to one side.

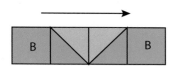

2. Sew together 4 patches. Press seams in opposite direction.

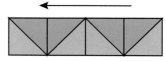

3. Sew together 4 patches. Press seams in same direction as row 1.

4. Sew together 2 patches and 2 pink print squares. Press seams in same direction as row 2.

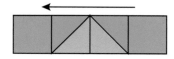

5. Sew rows together to complete block. Make a total of 9 blocks.

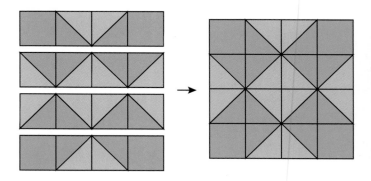

Finishing Your Quilt

1. Place blocks in three rows of three blocks referring to Layout. Sew blocks together in rows, then sew rows together. Press seams to one side.

2. Sew 2" x 32 ½" blue print strips to sides first; press seams toward border. Sew 2" x 35 ½" blue print strips to top and bottom; press seams toward border strips.

3. Sew 3 ½" x 35 ½" pink print strips to sides; press seams toward border strips. Sew 3 ½" x 41 ½" pink print strips to top and bottom; press seam toward border strips.

4. Refer to Finishing Your Quilt, pages 58 to 61, to complete your quilt.

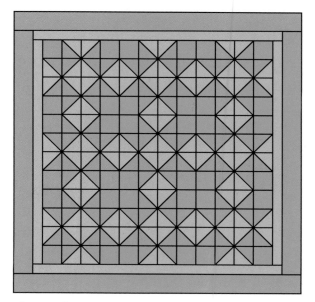

Layout

Whirling Pinwheels

Approximate Size 33" x 41"

If you have never made a quilt before, this is a great way to start. Although the quilt may be easy to piece, the final results are certain to delight that baby.

13

continued on page 14

Materials

¾ yd red print
1 ¼ yds blue print
¾ yd beige print
1 ¼ yds backing
batting

Patterns

(page 63)
A Triangle
B Square

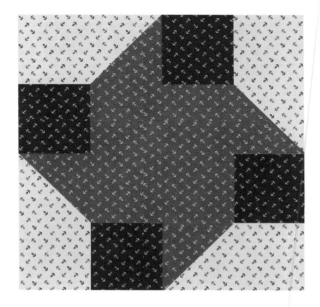

Cutting

Pinwheel Block (8" x 8" finished)

Note: *Refer to Templates, page 57, to make templates and cut fabric.*

(make 12)

48 A Triangles, red print
48 B Squares, red print
48 B Squares, blue print
48 A Triangles, beige print
48 B Squares, beige print

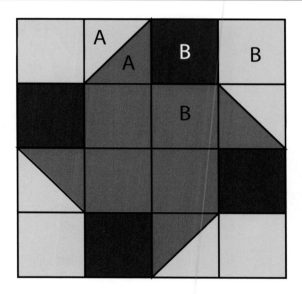

Finishing

2 strips, 2" x 32 ½", red print (first border-sides)
2 strips, 2" x 24 ½", red print (first border-top and bottom)
2 strips, 3 ½" x 35 ½", blue print (second border-sides)
2 strips, 3 ½" x 27 ½", blue print (second border-top and bottom)
4 squares, 2" x 2", beige print (cornerstones)
4 squares, 3 ½" x 3 ½", beige print (cornerstones)
6 strips, 2 ½"-wide, blue print (binding)

Instructions

Making the Block

Making the Patches

1. Sew a red print A Triangle to a beige print A Triangle; press seams to one side. Repeat for a total of 4 patches.

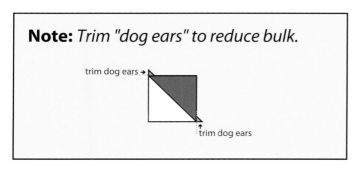

Note: *Trim "dog ears" to reduce bulk.*

trim dog ears →

↑ trim dog ears

Sewing the Rows

1. For row 1, sew together 1 beige print B Square, 1 patch, 1 blue print B Square and another beige print B Square. Press seams to one side.

2. For row 2, sew together a blue print B Square, 2 red print B Squares and 1 patch. Press seams in opposite direction.

3. For row 3, sew together 1 patch, 2 red print B Squares and 1 blue print B Square. Press seams in same direction as row 1.

4. For row 4, sew together 1 beige print B Square, 1 blue print B Square, 1 patch and another beige print B Square. Press seams

in same direction as row 2.

5. Sew rows together to complete block. Make a total of 12 blocks.

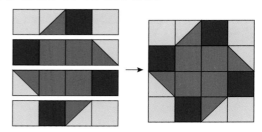

Finishing Your Quilt

1. Place blocks in four rows of three blocks referring to Layout. Sew blocks together in rows, then sew rows together. Press seams to one side.

2. Sew 2" x 32 ½" red print strips to sides first; press seams toward border. Sew 2" x 2" beige print squares to opposite sides of a 2" x 24 ½" red print strip; repeat. Press seams toward border strip. Sew to top and bottom of quilt; press seams toward border strips.

continued on page 16

3. Sew 3 ½" x 35 ½" blue print strips to sides; press seams toward border strips. Sew 3 ½" x 3 ½" beige print squares to opposite sides of a 3 ½" x 27 ½" blue print strip; repeat. Press seams toward blue print strip. Sew to top and bottom of quilt.

4. Refer to Finishing Your Quilt, pages 58 to 61, to complete your quilt.

Layout

Floating Hearts

Approximate Size 38" x 38"

A quilt with nine hearts: a wonderful way to express your love for that special baby.

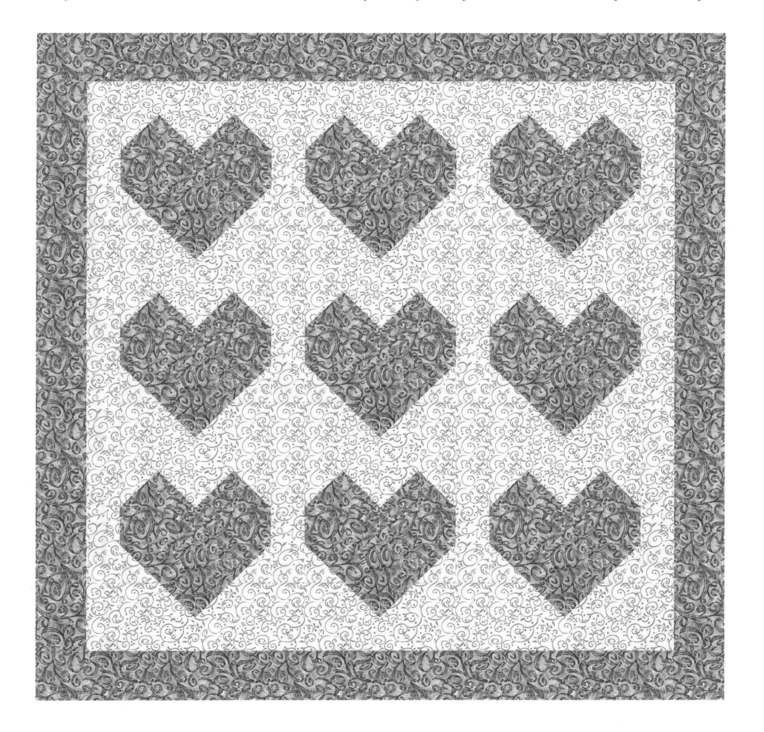

continued on page 18

Materials

1 ¼ yds pink print
1 yd aqua print
1 ¼ yds backing
batting

Patterns

(pages 62 and 63)
A Triangle
B Square
C Triangle

Cutting

Heart Block (8" x 8" finished)

Note: *Refer to Templates, page 57, to make templates and cut fabric.*

(make 9)

36 A Triangles, pink print
36 B Squares, pink print
18 C Triangles, pink print
36 A Triangles, aqua print
18 C Triangles, aqua print

Finishing

6 strips, 2 ½" x 8 ½", aqua print (sashing)
2 strips, 2 ½" x 28 ½", aqua print (sashing)

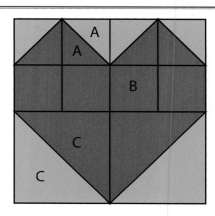

2 strips, 2 ½" x 28 ½", aqua print (first border-sides)

2 strips, 2 ½" x 32 ½", aqua print (first border-top and bottom)

2 strips, 3 ½" x 32 ½", pink print (second border-sides)

2 strips, 3 ½" x 38 ½", pink print (second border-top and bottom)

6 strips, 2 ½"-wide, pink print (binding)

Instructions

Making the Block

Making the Patches

1. Sew a pink print A Triangle to an aqua print A Triangle; press seams to one side. Repeat for a total of 4 small patches.

2. Sew a pink print C Triangle to an aqua print C Triangle; press seams to one side. Repeat for a total of 2 large patches.

Sewing the Rows

1. Sew together 4 small patches. Press seams to one side.

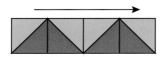

2. Sew together 4 pink print B Squares. Press seams in opposite direction.

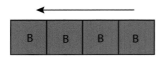

3. Sew together 2 large patches. Press seams in same direction as row 1.

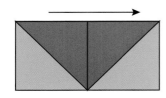

4. Sew rows together to complete block. Make a total of 9 blocks.

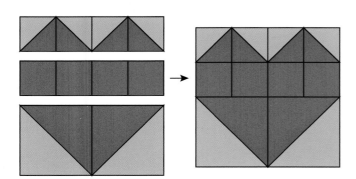

Finishing Your Quilt

1. Sew 3 Heart blocks with 2 ½" x 8 ½" aqua print strips in between. Repeat for 3 rows.

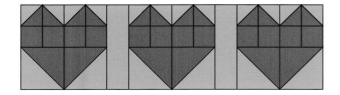

2. Sew the rows together with the 2 ½" x 28½" aqua strips in between.

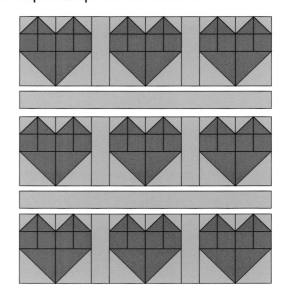

3. Sew 2 ½" x 28 ½" aqua print strips to sides; press seams toward border strips. Sew 2 ½" x 32 ½" aqua print strips to top and bottom. Press seams toward border strips.

4. Add 3 ½" x 32 ½" pink print border strips to sides and 3 ½" x 38 ½" pink print strips to top and bottom.

5. Refer to Finishing Your Quilt, pages 58 to 61, to complete your quilt.

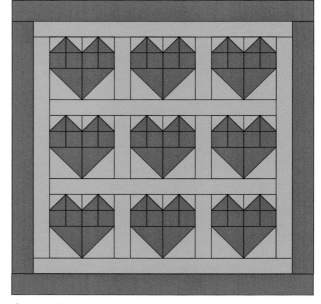

Layout

Baby's Log Cabin

Approximate Size 32" x 32"

This clever quilt takes a simple Log Cabin block, adds two easy-to-make borders, and turns it all into a delightful quilt for a happy baby.

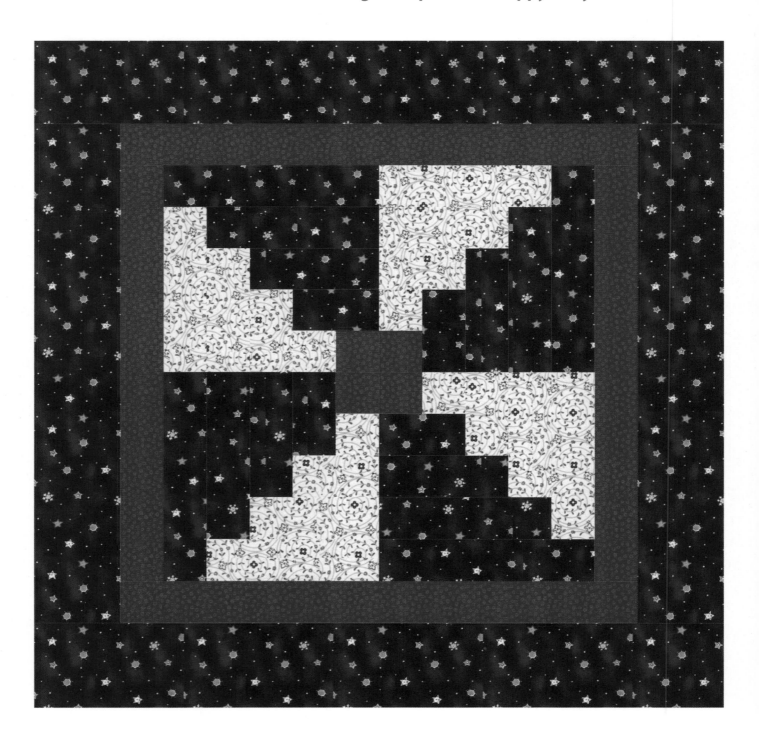

Materials

1 ¼ yds dk blue print
⅓ yd lt blue print
½ yd red print
1 yd backing
batting

Patterns

(pages 62 and 63)
B Square
D, E, F, G Rectangles

Cutting

Log Cabin Block (10" x 10" finished)

Note: *Refer to Templates, page 57, to make templates and cut fabric.*

(make 4)

4 B Squares each, red print and lt blue print
4 D Rectangles each, lt blue print and dk blue print
4 E Rectangles each, lt blue print and dk blue print
4 F Rectangles each, lt blue print and dk blue print
4 G Rectangles, dk blue print

Finishing

2 strips, 2 ½" x 20 ½", red print (first border-sides)
2 strips, 2 ½" x 24 ½", red print (first border-top and bottom)
2 strips, 4 ½" x 24 ½", dk blue print (second border-sides)
2 strips, 4 ½" x 32 ½", dk blue print (second border-top and bottom)
4 strips, 2 ½"-wide, dk blue print (binding)

Instructions

Making the Block

1. Sew a red print B Square to lt blue print B Square; press seam toward lt blue.

2. Turn sewn squares clockwise and place dk blue print D Rectangle right side down on squares; sew. Press seam toward dk blue Rectangle.

continued on page 22

3. Turn piece clockwise and place lt blue D Rectangle right side down; sew. Press seam toward lt blue Rectangle.

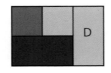

4. Turn piece counterclockwise and place dk blue E Rectangle right side down; sew. Press seam toward dk blue Rectangle.

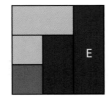

5. Turn piece clockwise and place lt blue print E Rectangle right side down; sew. Press seam toward lt blue Rectangle.

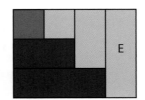

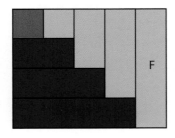

6. Turn piece counterclockwise and place dk blue F Rectangle right side down; sew. Press seam toward dk blue Rectangle.

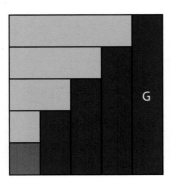

7. Turn piece clockwise and place lt blue F Rectangle right side down; sew. Press seam toward lt blue Rectangle.

8. Turn piece counterclockwise and place dk blue G Rectangle right side down; sew. Press seam toward dk blue Rectangle to complete block.

Repeat for a total of 4 blocks.

Finishing Your Quilt

1. Referring to Layout, sew Log Cabin blocks in pairs, then sew pairs together.

2. Sew 2 ½" x 20 ½" red print strips to sides of quilt top; press seams toward border.

3. Sew 2 ½" x 24 ½" red print strips to top and bottom; press seams toward red print strips.

4. Sew 4 ½" x 24 ½" dk blue print strips to sides of quilt; press seams toward dk blue strips.

5. Sew 4 ½" x 32 ½" dk blue strips to top and bottom; press seams toward dk blue strips.

6. Refer to Finishing Your Quilt, pages 58 to 61, to complete your quilt.

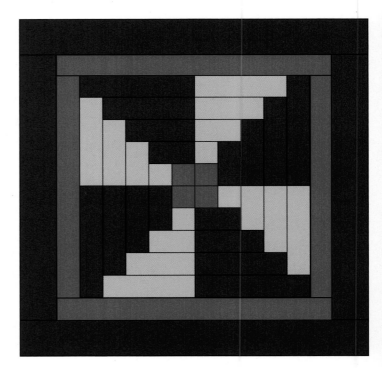

Layout

Baby's Pal

Approximate Size 42" x 42"

It doesn't matter if baby's pal is a pet frog (as shown here), this quilt will delight the recipient. The only chore will be to find a novelty print with the proper animal.

continued on page 24

Materials

¾ yd novelty print

1 ½ yds med blue print

1 yd dk blue print

1 ¼ yds backing

batting

Patterns

(pages 62-64)

I Square

D Rectangle

A Triangle

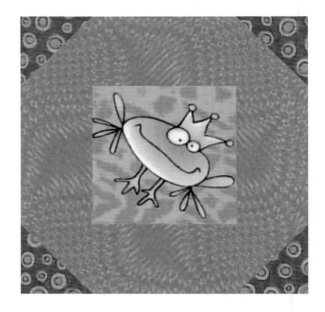

Cutting

Note: *Refer to Templates, page 57, to make templates and cut fabric.*

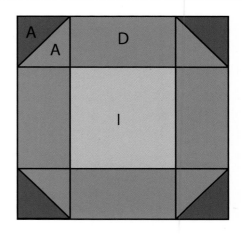

Snowball Block (8" x 8" finished)

(make 16)

*16 I Squares novelty print

64 D Rectangles, med blue print

64 A Triangles, med blue print

64 A Triangles, dk blue print

Finishing

2 strips, 1 ½" x 32 ½", dk blue print (first border-sides)

2 strips, 1 ½" x 34 ½", dk blue print (first border-top and bottom)

2 strips, 4 ½" x 34 ½", med blue print (second border-sides)

2 strips, 4 ½" x 42 ½", med blue print (second border-top and bottom)

4 strips, 2 ½"-wide, dk blue print (binding)

* Fussy cut the center I Square. Make your template from clear template plastic referring to Making the Template, page 57. Place template on fabric, centering the image you would like to use (photographed quilt shows a frog). Trace around template; cut out around traced line. Repeat for all squares.

Instructions

Making the Block

1. Sew a med blue A Triangle to a dk blue A Triangle; press seam toward dk blue A Triangle. Make a total of 4 patches.

2. Sew a patch to each end of a med blue D Rectangle; press seam toward D Rectangle. Repeat.

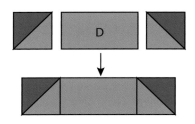

3. Sew a med blue D Rectangle to opposite sides of novelty print I Square. Press seams toward med blue print Rectangle.

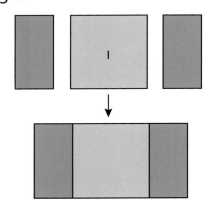

4. Sew strips from steps 2 and 3 together to complete block. Make a total of 16 blocks.

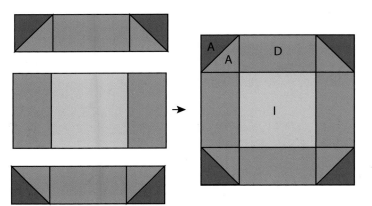

Finishing Your Quilt

1. Sew Snowball blocks together in 4 rows of 4 blocks. Press seams for rows in opposite directions.

2. Sew 1 ½" x 32 ½" dk print strips to sides of quilt; press seams toward border. Sew 1 ½" x 34 ½" dk blue print strips to top and bottom.

3. Sew 4 ½" x 34 ½" med print strips to sides of quilt; press seams toward dk blue strips.

4. Sew 4 ½" x 42 ½" dk blue strips to top and bottom of quilt. Press seams toward border strips.

5. Refer to Finishing Your Quilt, pages 58 to 61, to complete your quilt.

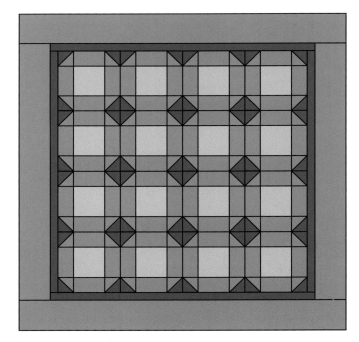

Layout

Sailing, Sailing...

Approximate Size 34" x 34"

*Four red sailboats make their way across this quilt,
carrying a sleepy baby to dreamland.*

Materials

¼ yd lt blue
1 yd med blue print
½ yd red print
½ yd beige print
1 ⅛ yds backing
batting

Patterns

(page 63)
A Triangle
B Square

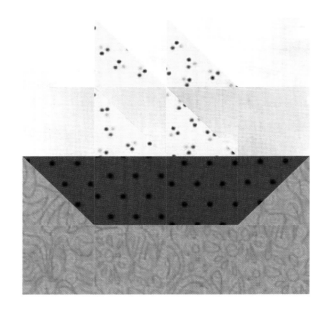

Cutting

Note: *Refer to Templates, page 57, to make templates and cut fabric.*

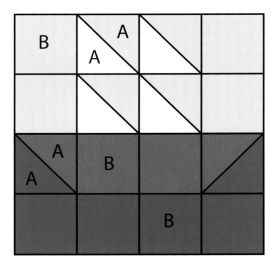

Sailboat Block (8" x 8" finished)

(make 4)

16 A Triangles, lt blue
16 B Squares, lt blue
8 A Triangles, med blue print
16 B Squares, med blue print
8 A Triangles, red print
8 B Squares, red print
16 A Triangles, beige print

Finishing

12 strips, 2 ½" x 8 ½", red print (sashing)
9 squares, 2 ½" x 2 ½", med blue print (cornerstones)
2 strips, 2 ½" x 22 ½", beige print (first border-sides)
2 strips, 2 ½" x 26 ½", beige print (first border-top and bottom)
2 strips, 4 ½" x 26 ½", med blue print (second border-sides)
2 strips, 4 ½" x 34 ½", med blue print (second border-top and bottom)
4 strips, 2 ½"-wide, med blue print (binding)

continued on page 28

Instructions

Making the Block

Making the Patches

1. Sew a beige print A Triangle to a lt blue A Triangle; press seam to one side. Repeat for a total of 4 patches.

2. Sew two patches together; then sew a lt blue B Square to each end for row 1. Repeat for row 2.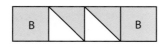

3. Sew a med blue A Triangle to a red print A Triangle; press seam to one side. Repeat for another patch.

4. Sew a pair of red print B Squares together; sew a patch to each end for row 3.

5. Sew four med blue B Squares together for row 4.

6. Sew rows 1, 2, 3 and 4 together to complete block. Make a total of 4 blocks.

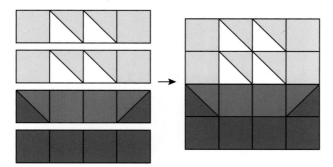

Finishing Your Quilt

1. Sew two Sailboat blocks together with a 2 ½" x 8 ½" red print strip in between; sew a red print strip on each end. Press seams toward red print strip. Repeat for another row.

2. Sew two 2 ½" x 8 ½" red print strips with a med blue 2 ½" square in between; sew a med blue square on each end. Press seams toward red print strips. Repeat for two more rows.

3. Sew block and sashing rows together. Press seams to one side.

4. Sew 2 ½" x 22 ½" beige strips to sides of quilt top; press seams toward border. Sew 2 ½" x 26 ½" beige print strips to top and bottom of quilt; press seams toward border.

5. Sew 4 ½" x 26 ½" med blue strips to sides of quilt top; press seams toward border. Sew 4 ½" x 34 ½" med blue strips to sides of quilt top; press seams toward border.

6. Refer to Finishing Your Quilt, pages 58 to 61, to complete your quilt.

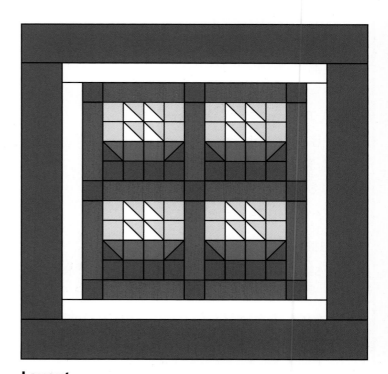

Layout

Find the Pinwheels

Approximate Size 33" x 41"

*What child wouldn't delight in locating all of the pinwheels
floating across this delightful quilt.*

continued on page 30

Materials

1 ½ yds red print
½ yd blue print
⅞ yd yellow print
½ yd beige print
1 ¼ yds backing
batting

Pattern

(page 63)
A Triangle

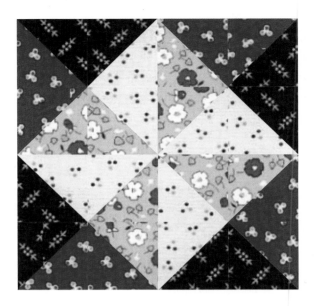

Cutting

Note: *Refer to Templates, page 57, to make templates and cut fabric.*

Pinwheel Block (8" x 8" finished)
(make 12)

96 A Triangles, red print
96 A Triangles, blue print
96 A Triangles, yellow print
96 A Triangles, beige print

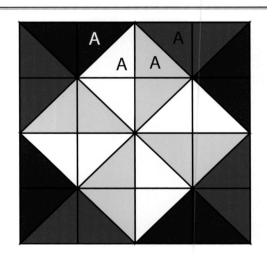

Finishing

2 strips, 2" x 32 ½", yellow print (first border-sides)
2 strips, 2" x 27 ½", yellow print (first border-top and bottom)
2 strips, 3 ½" x 35 ½", red print (second border-sides)
2 strips, 3 ½" x 33 ½", red print (second border-top and bottom)
4 strips, 2 ½"-wide, red print (binding)

Instructions

Making the Block

Making the Patches

1. Sew a red print A Triangle to a blue print A Triangle; press seam toward one side. Make a total of 4 A patches.

2. Sew a blue A Triangle to a beige print A Triangle; press seam toward one side. Make a total of 4 B patches.

 3. Sew a yellow A Triangle to a red print A Triangle; press seam to one side. Make a total of 4 C patches.

 4. Sew a yellow print A Triangle to a beige print A Triangle; press seam to one side. Make a total of 4 D patches.

5. Sew an A patch to a B patch; press seam to one side. Sew a C patch to a D patch; press seam to opposite side. Sew the rows together. Make a total of 4 pieced squares.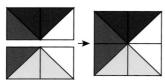

6. Sew two pieced squares together; repeat. Press seams to one side.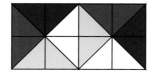

7. Sew the rows together to complete the block. Make a total of 12 blocks.

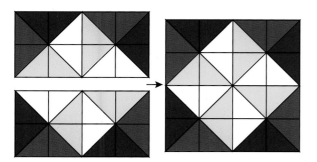

Finishing Your Quilt

1. Referring to layout, sew Pinwheel blocks together in four rows of three blocks; press seams for rows in opposite directions.

2. Sew rows together; press seams in one direction.

3. Sew 2" x 32 ½" yellow print strips to sides of quilt top; press seams toward border. Sew 2" x 27 ½" yellow print strips to top and bottom of quilt.

4. Sew 3 ½" x 35 ½" red print strips to sides of quilt top; press seams toward border. Sew 3 ½" x 33 ½" red print strips to top and bottom of quilt top; press seams toward border.

5. Refer to Finishing Your Quilt, pages 58 to 61, to complete your quilt.

Layout

31

Twirling Flowers

Approximate Size 33" x 33"

Bring the garden into the house with these flowers dancing in this quilt.

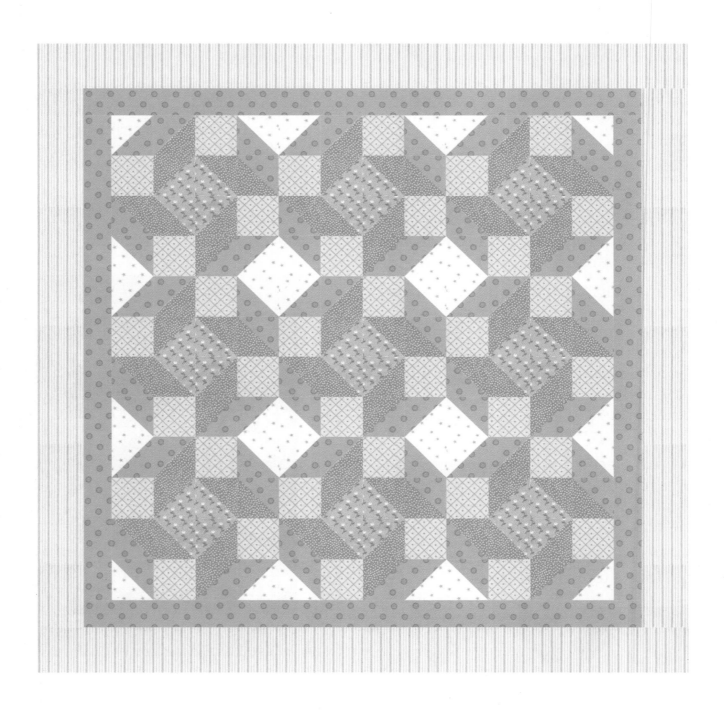

Materials

¼ yd lt pink print
¼ yd med pink print
⅝ yd dk pink print
¼ yd white print
¾ yd green print
¼ yd pink stripe
1 yd backing
batting

Patterns

(page 63)
A Triangle
B Square

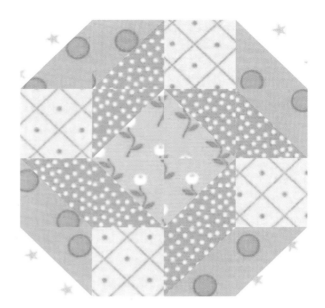

Cutting

Note: *Refer to Templates, page 57, to make templates and cut fabric.*

Twirling Flower Block (8" x 8" finished)
(make 9)

36 B Squares, lt pink print
36 A Triangles, med pink print
72 A Triangles, dk pink print
36 A Triangles, white print
72 A Triangles, green print

Finishing

2 strips, 2" x 24 ½", green print (first border-sides)
2 strips, 2" x 27 ½", geen print (first border-top and bottom)
*2 strips, 3 ½" x 27 ½", pink stripe (second border-sides)
*2 strips, 3 ½" x 33 ½", pink stripe (second border-top and bottom)
4 strips, 2 ½"-wide, lt pink print (binding)

* In order to have the stripes going in the same direction, cut the side border strips first along the lengthwise grain of the fabric; then cut the top and bottom border strips.

continued on page 34

Instructions

Making the Block

Making the Patches

1. Sew a white print A Triangle to a green print A Triangle; press seam to one side. Make a total of 4 A patches.

2. Sew a green print A Triangle to a dk pink print A Triangle; press seams to one side. Make a total of 4 B patches.

3. Sew a dk pink print A Triangle to a med pink print A Triangle; press seam to one side. Make a total of 4 C patches.

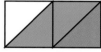
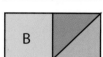
4. Sew a patch A to a patch B; press seam to one side. Sew a lt pink B Square to a C patch; press seam to one side.

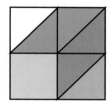
5. Sew rows from step 4 together to make a pieced square; press seam to one side. Repeat for a total of 4 pieced squares.

6. Sew pieced squares together in pairs, then sew rows together to complete block. Make a total of 9 blocks.

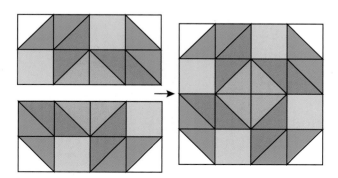

Finishing Your Quilt

1. Referring to the layout, sew blocks together in three rows of three blocks; press seams for rows in opposite directions. Sew rows together.

2. Sew 2" x 24 ½" green print strips together; press seams toward border. Sew 2" x 27 ½" green print strips to top and bottom of quilt top; press seams toward border.

3. Sew 3 ½" x 27 ½" pink stripe strips to sides of quilt top; press seam toward border. Sew 3 ½" x 33 ½" pink stripe strips to top and bottom of quilt top. **Note:** *If you use a stripe print, be sure to cut strips so they are going the same direction when sewn to the quilt top.*

4. Refer to Finishing Your Quilt, pages 58 to 61, to complete your quilt.

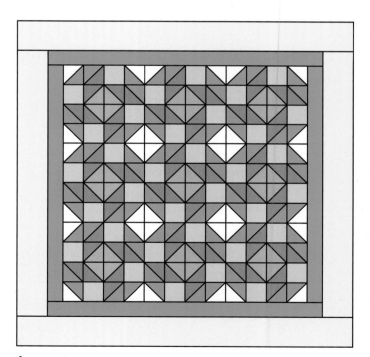

Layout

Star Galaxy

Approximate Size 36" x 44"

Stars float across this quilt, and in addition, red pinwheels magically appear when the blocks are sewn together.

continued on page 36

Materials

⅝ yd red print

1 ½ yds black print

¾ yd dk blue print

⅝ yd gray print

⅝ yd lt blue print

⅝ yd med blue print

1 ½ yds backing

batting

Patterns

(page 63)

A Triangle

Cutting

Note: *Refer to Templates, page 57, to make templates and cut fabric.*

Star Block
(8" x 8" finished)

(make 12)

48 A Triangles, red

96 A Triangles, black

96 A Triangles, dk blue

48 A Triangles, gray

48 A Triangles, lt blue

48 A Triangles, med blue

Finishing

4 strips, 2 ½" x 32 ½", red (first border)

4 strips, 4 ½" x 36 ½", black (second border)

4 squares, 2 ½" x 2 ½", dk blue (corner squares)

4 squares, 4 ½" x 4 ½", dk blue (corner squares)

4 strips, 2 ½"-wide, black (binding)

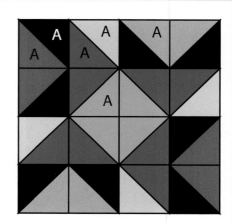

Instructions

Making the Block

1. Sew a red A Triangle to a black A Triangle; press seam to one side. Make a total of 4 A patches.

2. Sew a dk blue A Triangle to a lt blue A Triangle; press seam to one side. Make a total of 4 B patches.

3. Sew a black A Triangle to a gray A Triangle; press seam to one side. Make a total of 4 C patches.

4. Sew a dk blue A Triangle to a med blue A Triangle; press seam to one side. Make a total of 4 D patches.

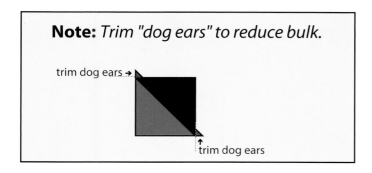

Note: *Trim "dog ears" to reduce bulk.*

trim dog ears →

trim dog ears

5. For row 1, sew an A patch, B patch and 2 C patches together.

6. For row 2, sew an A patch, 2 D patches and a B patch together.

7. For row 3, sew a B patch, 2 D patches and an A patch together.

8. For row 4, sew 2 C patches, a B patch and an A patch together.

9. Press seams for rows 1 and 3 in one direction and for rows 2 and 4 in opposite direction. Sew rows together to complete block. Make a total of 12 blocks.

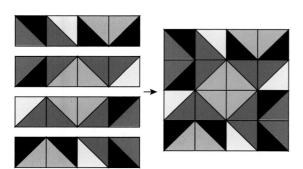

Finishing Your Quilt

1. Referring to layout, sew blocks together in four rows of three blocks. Press seams for rows in alternating directions. Sew rows together.

2. Sew 2 ½" x 32 ½" red strips to sides of quilt top. Press seams toward border.

3. Sew a 2 ½" dk blue square to each end of remaining 2 ½" x 32 ½" red strips; press seams toward red strip. Sew to top and bottom of quilt top; press seams toward border.

4. Sew 4 ½" x 36 ½" black strip to sides of quilt top; press seams toward border.

5. Sew 4 ½" dk blue square to each end of remaining 4 ½" x 36 ½" black strips; press seams toward black strip. Sew to top and bottom of quilt top; press seams toward border.

6. Refer to Finishing Your Quilt, pages 58 to 61, to complete your quilt.

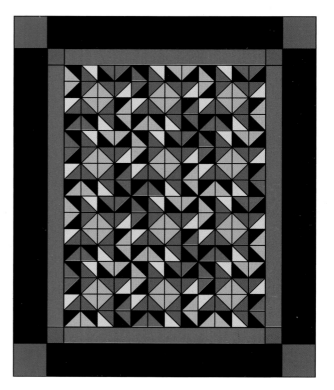

Layout

37

Blocks All Stacked Up

Approximate Size 33" x 33"

Here's the perfect quick and easy gift for that brand new baby that will be sure to please while it keeps the little one warm.

Materials

¼ yd pink print
1 yd aqua print
½ yd yellow print
1 yd backing
batting

Patterns

(pages 62 and 63)
B Square
H Square

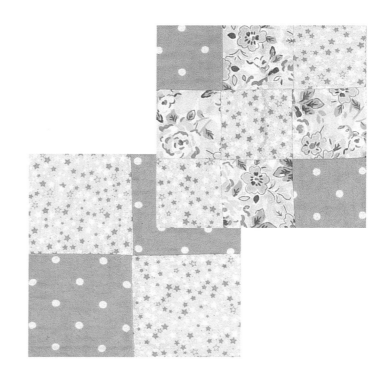

Cutting

Note: *Refer to Templates, page 57, to make templates and cut fabric.*

Nine Patch Block (6" x 6" finished)

(make 8)

24 B Squares, pink print
16 B Squares, aqua print
32 B Squares, yellow print

Four Patch Block (6" x 6" finished)

(make 8)

16 H Squares, pink print
16 H Squares, aqua print

Finishing

2 strips, 2" x 24 ½", aqua print (first border-sides)
2 strips, 2" x 27 ½", aqua print (first border-top and bottom)
2 strips, 3 ½" x 27 ½", yellow print (second border-sides)
2 strips, 3 ½" x 33 ½", yellow print (second border-top and bottom)
4 strips, 2 ½"-wide, yellow print (binding)

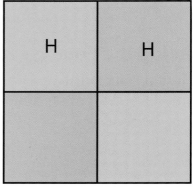

continued on page 40

Instructions

Making the Nine Patch

1. For row 1, sew an aqua print B Square and a pink print B Square to opposite sides of a yellow print B Square; press seams toward yellow print square. Repeat for row 3.

2. For row 2, sew a yellow print B Square to opposite sides of a pink print B Square; press seams toward yellow squares.

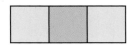

3. Sew rows 1, 2 and 3 together to complete Nine Patch. Press seams to one side. Make a total of 8 Nine Patch blocks.

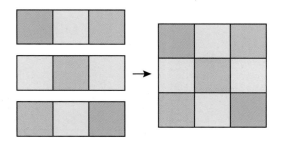

Making the Four Patch

1. Sew a pink print H Square to an aqua print H Square; press seam toward pink print. Repeat.

2. Sew the two pairs of squares together to complete Four Patch. Press seam to one side. Make a total of 8 Four Patch blocks.

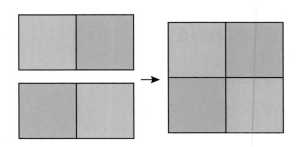

Finishing Your Quilt

1. Referring to layout, place blocks in four rows of four blocks. Sew blocks together in rows, then sew rows together.

2. Sew 2" x 24 ½" aqua print strips to sides of quilt top; press seam toward border. Sew 2" x 27 ½" aqua print strips to top and bottom of quilt top; press seams toward border.

3. Sew 3 ½" x 27 ½" yellow print strips to sides of quilt; press seams toward border. Sew 3 ½" x 33 ½" yellow print strips to top and bottom of quilt; press seams toward border.

4. Refer to Finishing Your Quilt, pages 58 to 61, to complete your quilt.

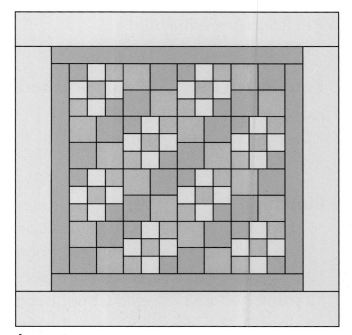

Layout

Starry Stars

Approximate Size 45" x 45"

As baby heads off for dreamland, he (or she) will be wrapped in stars in this quilt.

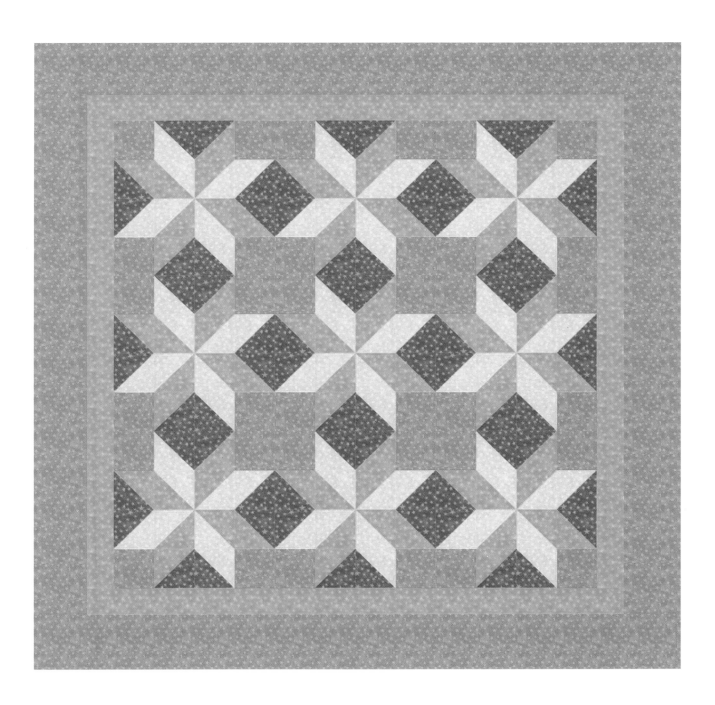

continued on page 42

Materials

1 yd turquoise print
⅝ yd purple print
⅝ yd yellow print
⅝ yd green print
1 ½ yd backing
batting

Patterns

(page 63)
A Triangle
B Square

Cutting

Note: *Refer to Templates, page 57, to make templates and cut fabric.*

Star Block (8" x 8" finished)

(make 9)

36 B Squares, turquoise print
72 A Triangles, purple print
72 A Triangles, yellow print
72 A Triangles, green print

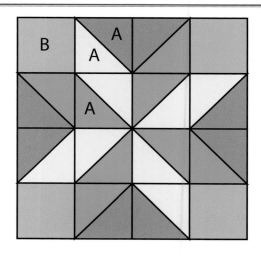

Finishing

2 strips, 2" x 36 ½", green print (first border- sides)
2 strips, 2" x 39 ½", green print (first border-top and bottom)
2 strips, 3 ½" x 39 ½", turquoise print (second border-sides)
2 strips, 3 ½" x 45 ½", turquoise print (second border-top and bottom)
4 strips, 2 ½"-wide, turquoise print (binding)

Instructions

Making the Block

1. Sew a purple print A Triangle to a yellow print A triangle; press seam to one side. Repeat for 3 more patches.

 2. Sew a purple print A Triangle to a green print A Triangle; press seam to one side. Repeat for 3 more patches.

3. Sew a green print A Triangle to a yellow print A Triangle; press seam to one side. Repeat for 3 more patches.

4. Sew a turquoise print B Square to a patch from step 1. Press seam to one side. Sew a patch from step 2 to a patch from step 3; press seam in opposite direction. Sew rows together. Repeat for 3 more sections.

5. Sew two sections together; repeat.

6. Sew halves together to complete block. Make a total of 9 blocks.

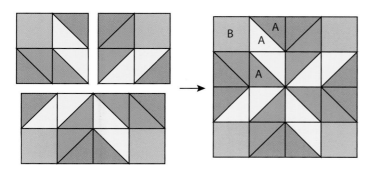

Finishing Your Quilt

1. Referring to layout, place blocks in three rows of three blocks. Sew blocks together in rows; then sew rows together.

2. Sew 2" x 36 ½" green print strips to sides of quilt top; press seam toward border. Sew 2" x 39 ½" green print strips to top and bottom of quilt top; press seams toward border.

3. Sew 3 ½" x 39 ½" turquoise print strips to sides of quilt; press seams toward border. Sew 3 ½" x 45 ½" turquoise print strips to top and bottom of quilt; press seams toward border.

4. Refer to Finishing Your Quilt, pages 58 to 61, to complete your quilt.

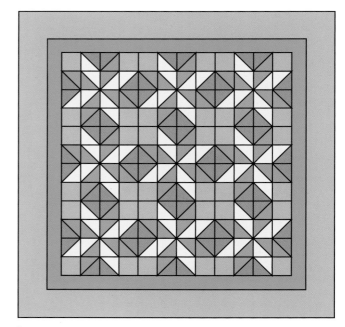

Layout

Purple Chain

Approximate Size 42" x 42"

The construction of this clever quilt is so quick and easy you'll be able to complete it for baby in record time.

Materials

1 ¼ yds lt purple print
¾ yd med purple print
½ yd dk purple print
1 ¼ yds backing
batting

Patterns

(pages 62 and 64)
H Square
J Rectangle

Cutting

Note: *Refer to Templates, page 57, to make templates and cut fabric.*

Chain Block (12" x 12" finished)

(make 9)

36 J Rectangles, lt purple print
36 H Squares, med purple print
36 H Squares, dk purple print

Finishing

4 strips, 3 ½" x 36 ½", lt purple print (border)
2 squares, 3 ½" x 3 ½", med purple print (cornerstones)
2 squares, 3 ½" x 3 ½", dk purple print (cornerstones)
4 strips, 2 ½"-wide, med purple print (binding)

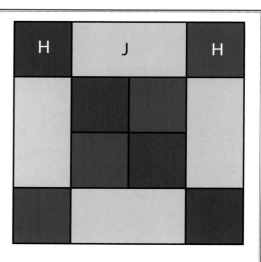

continued on page 46

Instructions

Making the Block

1. For row 1, sew a dk purple and a med purple H Square to each end of a lt purple J Rectangle. Press seams toward lt purple. Repeat for row 3.

2. For row 2, sew a dk purple and med purple H Square together; press seam toward dk purple. Repeat.

3. Sew the pairs of squares together to form a four patch.

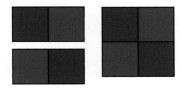

4. Sew a lt purple J Rectangle to opposite sides of four patch; press seams toward lt purple to complete row 2.

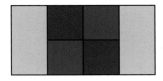

5. Sew rows together to complete block. Make a total of 9 blocks.

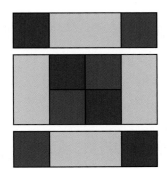
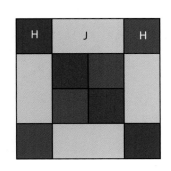

Finishing Your Quilt

1. Referring to layout, place blocks in three rows of three blocks. Sew blocks together in rows, then sew rows together.

2. Sew 3 ½" x 36 ½" lt purple print strips to sides of quilt top; press seam toward border.

3. Sew a 3 ½" dk purple square and a 3 ½" med purple square to opposite sides of 3 ½" x 36 ½" lt purple strip; press seams toward lt purple. Sew to top and bottom of quilt top. **Note:** *Be sure the dk purple and med purple squares follow the chain pattern color.*

4. Refer to Finishing Your Quilt, pages 58 to 61, to complete your quilt.

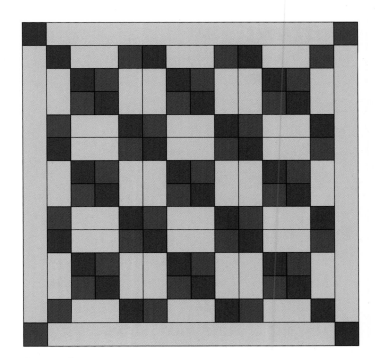

Layout

Baskets of Love

Approximate Size 38" x 46"

*A basket can hold many things, but the baskets in this quilt
are filled with love from the quilter.*

47

continued on page 48

Materials

1 ¼ yds pink print
⅝ yds turquoise print
1 ⅛ yds cream floral print
1 ¼ yds backing
batting

Patterns

(pages 62 and 63)
A Triangle
B Square
D Rectangle

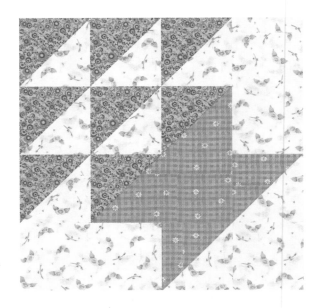

Cutting

Note: *Refer to Templates, page 57, to make templates and cut fabric.*

Basket Block (8" x 8" finished) *(make 12)*

96 A Triangles, pink print
96 A Triangles, cream floral print
48 A Triangles, turquoise print
12 B Squares, cream floral print
12 B Squares, turquoise print
24 D Rectangles, cream floral print

Finishing

2 strips, 2 ½" x 32 ½", cream floral print (first border-sides)
2 strips, 2 ½" x 28 ½", cream floral print (first border-top and bottom)
2 strips, 4 ½" x 36 ½", pink print (second border-sides)
2 strips, 4 ½" x 36 ½", pink print (second border-top and bottom)
4 strips, 2 ½"-wide, pink print (binding)

Instructions

Making the Block

1. Sew a pink print A Triangle to a cream floral A Triangle; press seam to one side. Repeat for a total of 6 patch 1.

2. Sew a pink print A Triangle to a turquoise print A Triangle; press seam to one side. Repeat for another patch 2.

3. Sew a turquoise print A Triangle to a cream floral A Triangle; press seam to one side. Repeat for another patch 3.

4. For row 1, sew three patch 1 together; press seams to one side.

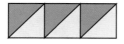

5. For row 2, sew two patch 1 and one patch 2 together; press seams to one side.

6. Sew rows 1 and 2 together.

7. Sew a cream floral D Rectangle to rows to complete upper half of block.

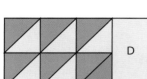

8. Sew a patch 1, patch 2, turquoise B Square and patch 3 together.

9. Sew a cream floral D Rectangle, patch 3 and cream floral B Square together.

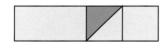

10. Sew strips from steps 8 and 9 together to complete lower half of block.

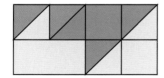

11. Sew upper and lower halves to complete block. Make a total of 12 blocks.

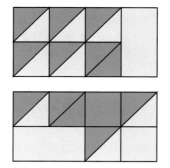
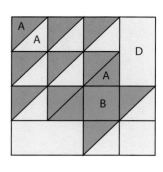

Finishing Your Quilt

1. Referring to layout, place blocks in three rows of four blocks. Sew blocks together in rows, then sew rows together.

2. Sew 2 ½" x 32 ½" cream floral strips to sides of quilt top; press seam toward border. Sew 2 ½" x 28 ½" cream floral strips to top and bottom of quilt top; press seams toward border.

3. Sew 4 ½" x 36 ½" pink print strips to sides of quilt; press seams toward border. Sew 4 ½" x 36 ½" pink print strips to top and bottom of quilt; press seams toward border.

4. Refer to Finishing Your Quilt, pages 58 to 61, to complete your quilt.

Layout

Two Terrific Triangles

Approximate Size 44" x 44"

*The perfect quilt that is fast and easy to make: one that uses only two
different blocks. Ready for that new baby in no time at all.*

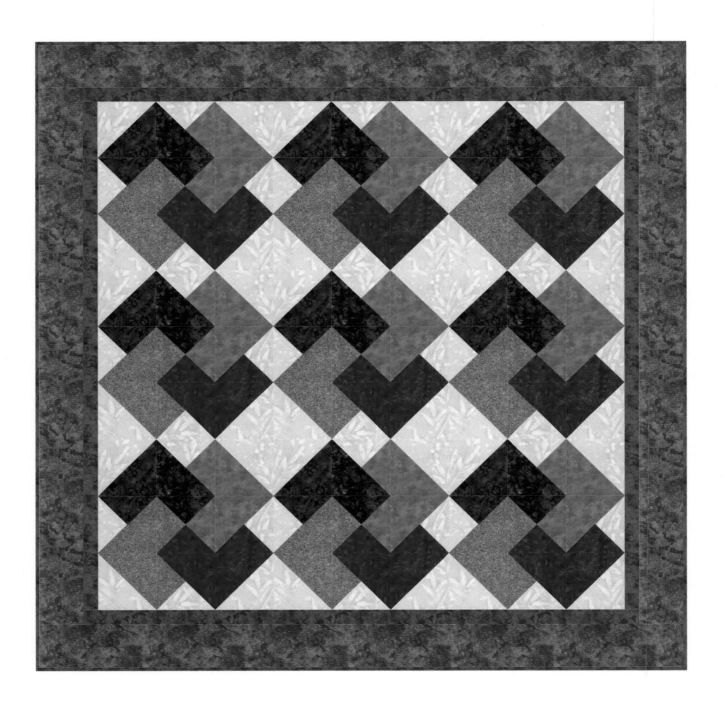

Materials

⅞ yd dk blue print

1 yd dk green print

⅝ yd orange print

⅝ yd red print

⅞ yd aqua print

1 ¼ yds backing

batting

Patterns

(pages 62 and 64)

C Triangle

K Triangle

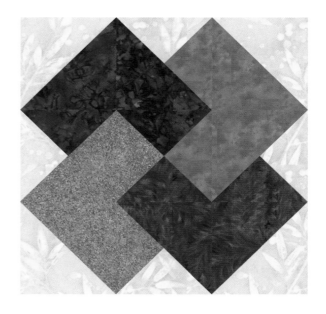

Cutting

Note: *Refer to Templates, page 57, to make templates and cut fabric.*

Triangle Block (12" x 12" finished) *(make 9)*

18 C Triangles, dk blue

18 K Triangles, dk blue

18 C Triangles, dk green

18 K Triangles, dk green

18 C Triangles, orange

18 K Triangles, orange

18 C Triangles, red

18 K Triangles, red

36 C Triangles, aqua

36 K Triangles, aqua

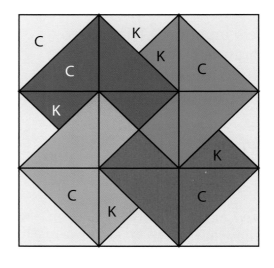

Finishing

2 strips, 1 ½" x 36 ½", dk blue (first border-sides)

2 strips, 1 ½" x 38 ½", dk blue (first border-top and bottom)

2 strips, 3 ½" x 38 ½", dk green (second border-sides)

2 strips, 3 ½" x 44 ½", dk green (second border-top and bottom)

4 strips, 2 ½"-wide, dk blue (binding)

continued on page 52

Instructions

Making the Block

1. Sew an aqua C Triangle to each of dk blue, dk green, orange and red C Triangle for patches 1, 2, 3, and 4.

2. Sew an aqua K Triangle to a dk green K Triangle; press seam to one side. Sew to dk blue C Triangle for patch 5.

3. Sew an aqua K Triangle to a red K Triangle; press seam to one side. Sew to dk green C Triangle for patch 6.

4. Sew an aqua K Triangle to an orange K Triangle; press seam to one side. Sew to red C Triangle for patch 7.

5. Sew an aqua K Triangle to a dk blue K Triangle; press seam to one side. Sew to orange C Triangle for patch 8.

6. Sew a dk blue and dk green K Triangle together; press seam to one side. Sew an orange and red K Triangle together; press seam to one side. Sew pairs together to make patch 9.

7. For row 1, sew patches 1, 5 and 2 together; press seams to one side.

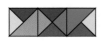

8. For row 2, sew patches 8, 9 and 6 together; press seams in opposite direction.

9. For row 3, sew patches 3, 7 and 4 together; press seams to one side.

10. Sew rows 1, 2 and 3 together to complete block. Make a total of 9 blocks.

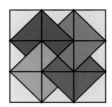

Finishing Your Quilt

1. Referring to layout, place blocks in three rows of three blocks. Sew together in rows, then sew rows together.

2. Sew 1 ½" x 36 ½" dk blue strips to sides of quilt; press seams toward border. Sew 1 ½" x 38 ½" dk blue strips to top and bottom of quilt; press seams toward border.

3. Sew 3 ½" x 38 ½" dk green strips to sides of quilt; press seams toward dk green border. Sew 3 ½" x 44 ½" dk green strips to top and bottom of quilt; press seams toward dk green border.

4. Refer to Finishing Your Quilt, pages 58 to 61, to complete your quilt.

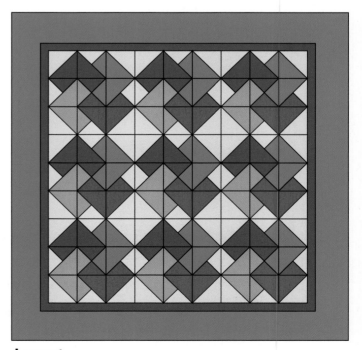

Layout

Pretty in Pink

Approximate Size 38" x 46"

A quilt that will be pretty in whatever color you choose, whether it's pink for a little girl or blue for a baby boy.

continued on page 54

Materials

⅞ yd pink print

1 ¼ yds red print

⅝ yd cream/pink print

1 ⅝ yds backing

batting

Patterns

(pages 63 and 64)

A Triangle

B Square

I Square

Cutting

Note: *Refer to Templates, page 57, to make templates and cut fabric.*

Pink Block (8" x 8" finished) *(make 12)*

96 A Triangles, pink print

96 A Triangles, cream/pink print

48 B Squares, red print

12 I Squares, cream/pink print

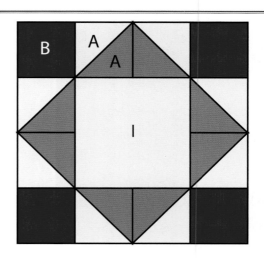

Finishing

2 strips, 3 ½" x 32 ½", pink print (first border-sides)

2 strips, 3 ½" x 30 ½", pink print (first border-top and bottom)

2 strips, 4 ½" x 38 ½", red print (second border-sides)

2 strips, 4 ½" x 38 ½", red print (second border-top and bottom)

4 strips, 2 ½"-wide, red print (binding)

Instructions

Making the Block

1. Sew a cream/pink A Triangle to pink print A Triangle; press seam toward pink print. Repeat for a total of 8 patches.

2. Sew two patches together; press seam to one side. Repeat for a total of 4 pairs of patches.

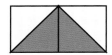

3. For row 1, sew a red print B Square to each end of pair of patches; press seams toward red print. Repeat for row 3.

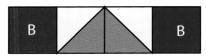

4. For row 2, sew a pair of patches to opposite sides of a cream/pink I Square; press seam toward cream/pink square.

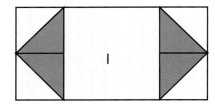

5. Sew rows 1, 2 and 3 together to complete block. Make a total of 12 blocks.

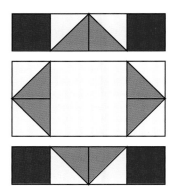
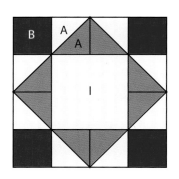

Finishing Your Quilt

1. Referring to Layout, place blocks in 4 rows of 3 blocks. Sew blocks together in rows, then sew rows together. Press seams for rows in opposite directions.

2. Sew 3 ½" x 32 ½" pink print strips to sides of quilt; press seams toward border. Sew 3 ½" x 30 ½" pink print strips to top and bottom of quilt; press seams toward border.

3. Sew 4 ½" x 38 ½" red print strips to sides of quilt; press seam toward red print border. Sew 4 ½" x 38 ½" red print strips to top and bottom of quilt; press seams toward red print border.

4. Refer to Finishing Your Quilt, pages 58 to 61, to complete your quilt.

Layout

General Directions

Fabric

For over a hundred years, quilts have been made with 100% cotton fabric, the choice for most quilters.

There are many properties in cotton that make it especially well-suited to quilt making. There is less distortion in cotton fabric, thereby affording the quilter greater security in making certain that even the smallest bits of fabric will fit together. Because a quilt block made of cotton can be ironed flat with a steam iron, a puckered area, created by mistake, can be fixed. The sewing machine needle can move through cotton with a great deal of ease when compared to some synthetic fabrics. While you may find that quilt artists today often use other kinds of fabric, to create the quilts quickly and accurately, 100% cotton is strongly recommended.

Cotton fabric today is produced in so many wonderful and exciting combinations of prints and solids that it is often difficult to pick colors for your quilt. We've chosen our favorite colors for these quilts, but don't be afraid to make your own choices.

For years, quilters were advised to prewash all of their fabric to test for colorfastness and shrinkage. Now most quilters don't bother to prewash all of their fabric but they do pretest it. Cut a strip about 2" wide from each piece of fabric that you will use in your quilt. Measure both the length and the width of the strip. Then immerse it in a bowl of very hot water, using a separate bowl for each piece of fabric. Be especially concerned about reds and dark blues because they have a tendency to bleed if the initial dyeing was not done properly. If it's one of your favorite fabrics that's bleeding, you might be able to salvage the fabric. Try washing the fabric in very hot water until you've washed out all of the excess dye. Unfortunately, fabrics that continue to bleed after they have been washed repeatedly will bleed forever. So eliminate them right at the start.

Now, take each one of the strips and iron them dry with a hot iron. Be especially careful not to stretch the strip. When the strips are completely dry, measure and compare them to your original strip. If all of your fabric is shrinking the same amount, you don't have to worry about uneven shrinkage in your quilt. When you wash the final quilt, the puckering that will result may give you the look of an antique quilt. If you don't want this look, you are going to have to wash and dry all of your fabric before you start cutting. Iron the fabric using some spray starch or sizing to give fabric a crisp finish.

If you are never planning to wash your quilt, i.e. your quilt is intended to be a wall hanging such as many of the quilts in this collection, you could eliminate the pre-testing process. You may run the risk, however, of some future relative to whom you have willed your quilts deciding that the wall hanging needs freshening by washing.

Before beginning to work, make sure that your fabric is absolutely square. If it is not, you will have difficulty cutting square pieces. Fabric is woven with crosswise and lengthwise threads. Lengthwise threads should be parallel to the selvage (that's the finished edge along the sides; sometimes the fabric company prints its name along the selvage), and crosswise threads should be perpendicular to the selvage. If fabric is off grain, you can usually straighten it by pulling gently on the true bias in the opposite direction to the off-grain edge. Continue doing this until the crosswise threads are at a right angle to the lengthwise threads.

Templates

All of the templates used to make the quilts in this book are on pages 62 to 64. Photocopy the templates needed for your project then glue the templates onto plastic or heavy cardboard. When you are certain that your glue has dried, cut out your templates. If your templates become worn, simply repeat the process. If you are planning to do your piecing by machine, cut out your templates on the solid line. If you are piecing by hand, cut out your templates on the broken lines. The seam allowances for hand piecing will be added later when you cut out the pieces. It's always a good idea to write the template's letter in the center of the template.

Cutting Fabric

For Machine Piecing

Lay the template (with the ¼" seam allowance added) on the wrong side of the fabric near the top left edge of the material but not on the selvage; place it so that as many straight sides of the piece as possible are parallel to the crosswise and lengthwise grain of the fabric. **Note:** *If there is an arrow on the pattern, place that edge on the straight (lengthwise or crosswise, not diagonal) grain of the fabric.* Trace around the template with a marking tool such as a hard lead pencil. This will be your cutting line; use a sharp scissors or a rotary cutter and cut accurately.

The traditional seam allowance in quilting is ¼" so be certain that you sew each seam with a ¼" seam allowance. After you have joined two pieces together, press the seams flat to one side, not open.

For Hand Piecing

Lay the template, cut on the broken lines, on the fabric as described above for Machine Piecing. Trace around the template with your marking tool. **This will be your stitching line.**

Now measure ¼" around this shape. With a ruler, draw this second line which is your cutting line. The seam allowance does not have to be perfect since it will not show, but the stitching line must be perfectly straight or the pieces will not fit together.

Making a Quilt

Sewing the Blocks Together

Once all of the blocks for your quilt have been made, place them on a flat surface such as a design wall or floor to decide on the best placement.

Sew the blocks together. You can do this by sewing the blocks in rows, then sewing the rows together; or, sew the blocks in pairs then sew pairs together. Continue sewing in pairs until entire quilt top is sewn together.

Adding Borders

Borders are usually added to a quilt sides first, then top and bottom.

Simple Borders

Step 1: Measure the quilt top lengthwise and cut two border strips to that length by the width measurement given in the project instructions. Strips may have to be pieced to achieve the correct length. To make the joining seam less noticeable, sew the strips together diagonally. Place two strips right sides together at right angles. Sew a diagonal seam. **(Diagram 1)**

Step 2: Trim excess fabric ¼" from stitching. **(Diagram 2)**

Step 3: Press seam open. **(Diagram 3)**

Step 4: Sew strips to the sides of the quilt. Press seam toward border. Now measure the quilt top crosswise, being sure to include the borders you have just added. Cut two border strips, following the width measurement given in the instructions.

Step 5: Add these borders to the top and bottom of the quilt. Repeat this process for any additional borders. Use the ¼" seam allowance at all times and press all of the seams to the darker side. Press the quilt top carefully.

Finishing Your Quilt

Attaching the Batting and Backing

There are a number of different types of batting on the market today including the new fusible battings that eliminate the need for basting. Your choice of batting will depend upon how you are planning to use your quilt. If the quilt is to serve as a wall hanging, you will probably want to use a thin cotton batting. A quilt made with a thin cotton or cotton/polyester blend works best for machine quilting. Very thick polyester batting should be used only for tied quilts.

The best fabric for quilt backing is 100% cotton fabric. If your quilt is larger than the available fabric you will have to piece your backing fabric. When joining the fabric, try not to have a seam going down the center. Instead cut off the selvages and make a center strip that is about 36" wide and have narrower strips at the sides. Seam the pieces together and carefully iron the seams open. (This is one of the few times in making a quilt that a seam should be pressed open.) Several fabric manufacturers are now selling fabric in 90" or 108"-widths for use as backing fabric.

It is a good idea to remove the batting from its wrapping 24 hours before you plan to use it and open it out to full size. You will find that the batting will now lie flat when you are ready to use it.

The batting and the backing should be cut about one to two inches larger on all sides than the quilt top. Place the backing wrong side up on a flat surface. Smooth out the batting on top of this, matching the outer edges. Center the quilt top, right side up, on top of the batting.

Now the quilt layers must be held together before quilting, and there are several methods for doing this:

Safety-pin Basting: Starting from the center and working toward the edges, pin through all layers at one time with large safety pins. The pins should be placed no more than 4" apart. As you work, think of your quilting plan to make sure that the pins will avoid prospective quilting lines.

Thread Basting: Baste the three layers together with long stitches. Start in the center and sew toward the edges in a number of diagonal lines.

Quilt-gun Basting: This handy trigger tool pushes nylon tags through all layers of the quilt. Start in the center and work toward the outside edges. The tags should be placed about 4" apart. You can sew right over the tags, which can then be easily removed by cutting them off with scissors.

Spray or Heat-Set Basting: Several manufacturers have spray adhesives available especially for quilters. Apply these products by following the manufacturers' directions. You might want to test these products before you use them to make sure that they meet your requirements.

Fusible Iron-on Batting: These battings are a wonderful new way to hold quilt layers together without using any of the other time-consuming methods of basting. Again, you will want to test these battings to be certain that you are happy with the results. Follow the manufacturers' directions.

Quilting

If you like the process of hand quilting, you can–of course–finish these projects by hand quilting. However, if you want to finish these quilts quickly, you will want to use a sewing machine for quilting.

If you have never used a sewing machine for quilting, you may want to find a book and read about the technique. You do not need a special machine for quilting. Just make sure that your machine has been oiled and is in good working condition.

If you are going to do machine quilting, you should invest in an even-feed foot. This foot is designed to feed the top and bottom layers of a quilt evenly through the machine. The foot prevents puckers from forming as you machine quilt. Use a fine transparent nylon thread in the top and regular sewing thread in the bobbin.

Quilting in the ditch is one of the easiest ways to machine quilt.

This is a term used to describe stitching along the seam line between two pieces of fabric. Using your fingers, pull the blocks or pieces apart slightly and machine stitch right between the two pieces. The stitching will look better if you keep the stitching to the side of the seam that does not have the extra bulk of the seam allowance under it. The quilting will be hidden in the seam.

Free-form machine quilting can be used to quilt around a design or to quilt a motif. The quilting is done with a darning foot and the feed dogs down on the sewing machine. It takes practice to master Free-form quilting because you are controlling the movement of the quilt under the needle rather than the sewing machine moving the quilt. You can quilt in any direction—up and down, side-to-side and even in circles—without pivoting the quilt around the needle. Practice this quilting method before trying it on your quilt.

Attaching the Continuous Machine Binding

Once the quilt has been quilted, it must be bound to cover the raw edges.

Step 1: Start by trimming the backing and batting even with the quilt top. Measure the quilt top and cut enough 2 ½" wide strips to go around all four sides of the quilt plus 12". Join the strips end to end with diagonal seams and trim the corners. **(Diagram 4)**

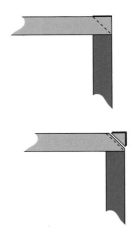

Press the seams open. **(Diagram 5)**

Step 2: Cut one end of the strip at a 45-degree angle and press under ¼". **(Diagram 6)**

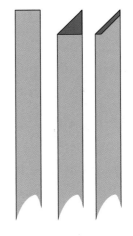

Step 3: Press entire strip in half lengthwise, wrong sides together. **(Diagram 7)**

Step 4: On the back of the quilt, position the binding in the middle of one side, keeping the raw edges together. Sew the binding to the quilt with the ¼" seam allowance, beginning about three inches below the folded end of the binding. **(Diagram 8)**

At the corner, stop ¼" from the edge of the quilt and backstitch.

Step 5: Fold binding away from quilt so it is at a right angle to edge just sewn. Then, fold the binding back on itself so the fold is on the quilt edge and the raw edges are aligned with the adjacent side of the quilt. Begin sewing at the quilt edge. **(Diagram 9)**

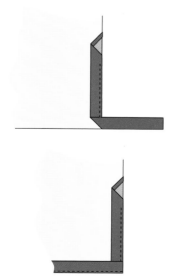

Step 6: Continue in the same way around the remaining sides of the quilt. Stop about 2" away from the starting point. Trim any excess binding and tuck it inside the folded end. Finish the stitching. **(Diagram 10)**

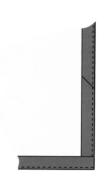

Step 7: Fold the binding to the front of the quilt so the seam line is covered; machine-stitch the binding in place on the front of the quilt. Use a straight stitch or tiny zigzag with invisible or matching thread. If you have a sewing machine that does embroidery stitches, you may want to use your favorite stitch.

Labeling Your Quilt

Always sign and date your quilt when finished. You can make a label by cross-stitching or embroidering or even writing on a label with a permanent marking pen on the back of your quilt. If you are friends with your computer, you can even create an attractive label on the computer.

Template Patterns

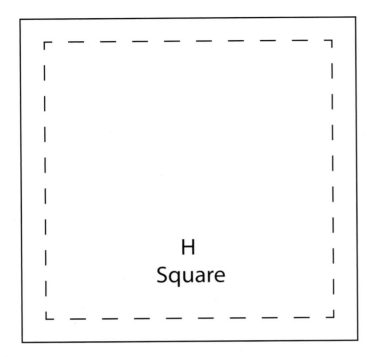

H
Square

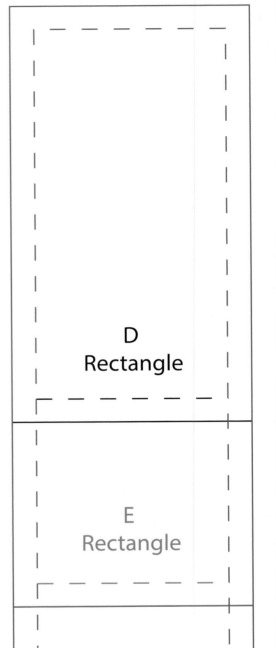

D
Rectangle

E
Rectangle

F
Rectangle

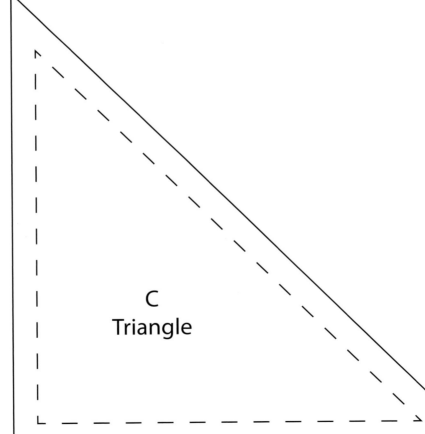

C
Triangle

Note: To make G Rectangle Template, trace outer line of each half pattern; place halves together at dashed red line. Be sure template measures 10 ½" in length for machine-pieced block and 10" for hand-pieced block.

G
Rectangle
(half 2)

G
Rectangle
(half 1)

Note: To make G Rectangle Template, trace outer line of each half pattern; place halves together at dashed red line. Be sure template measures 10 ½" in length for machine-pieced block and 10" for hand-pieced block.

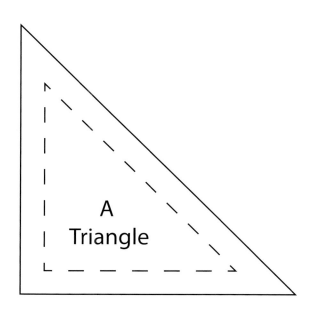

A
Triangle

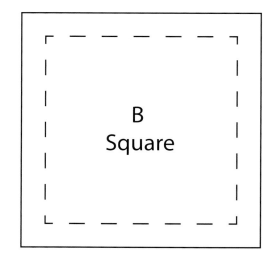

B
Square

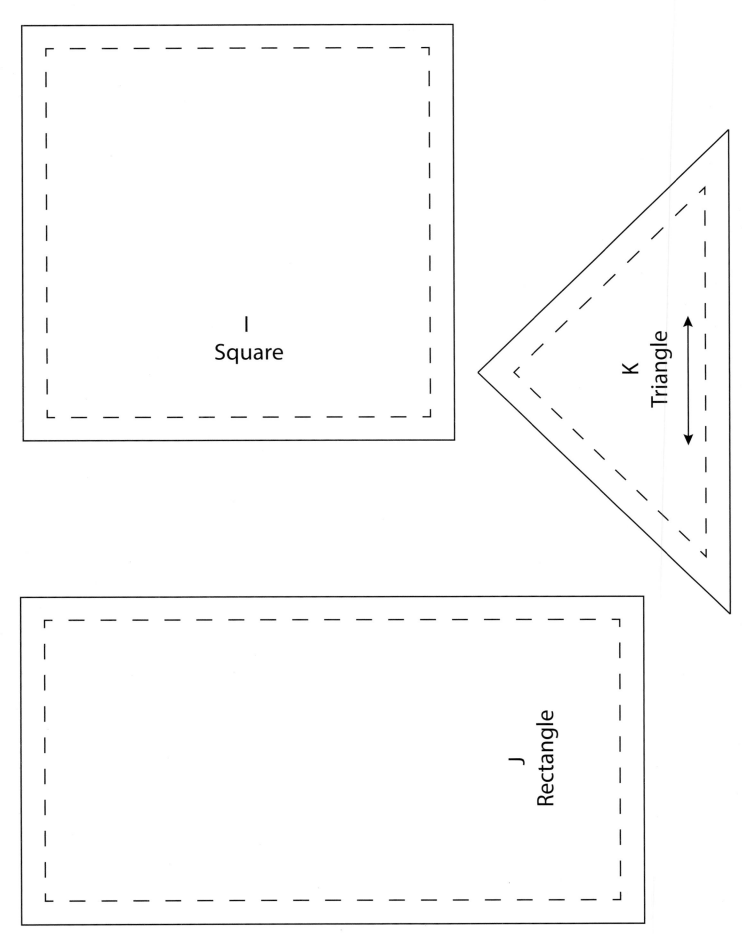

I
Square

K
Triangle

J
Rectangle